Christmas Dot to Dot For Adults from 150 to 547 Dots

By Laura's Dot to Dot Therapy

How To Use This Book

Hi! We're so glad you're a lover of puzzles and dot connecting- we are too!

Connecting the dots in this book is simple- just relax and follow the numbers in consecutive order, drawing a straight line between each one. Dot 1 will connect to dot 2 and so on and so forth until there are no more dots to connect. There's always another dot and you'll always find it. Connect every dot to discover the beautiful images they create.

In case you get lost or can't find a dot, never stress- there's an answer key at the back of the book that will show you exactly where each dot connects to the next. If you want to color your images, we encourage you to do so! Feel free to try all different colors and coloring mediums for your images!

If you find any errors or omissions in this book, email us at Laurasdottodot@gmail.com and please let us know! We want you to have the best dot to dot experience!

Image 1

Image 3

Image 4

Image 5

Image 7

Image 8

Image 9

Image 10

Image 11

Image 13

Image 18

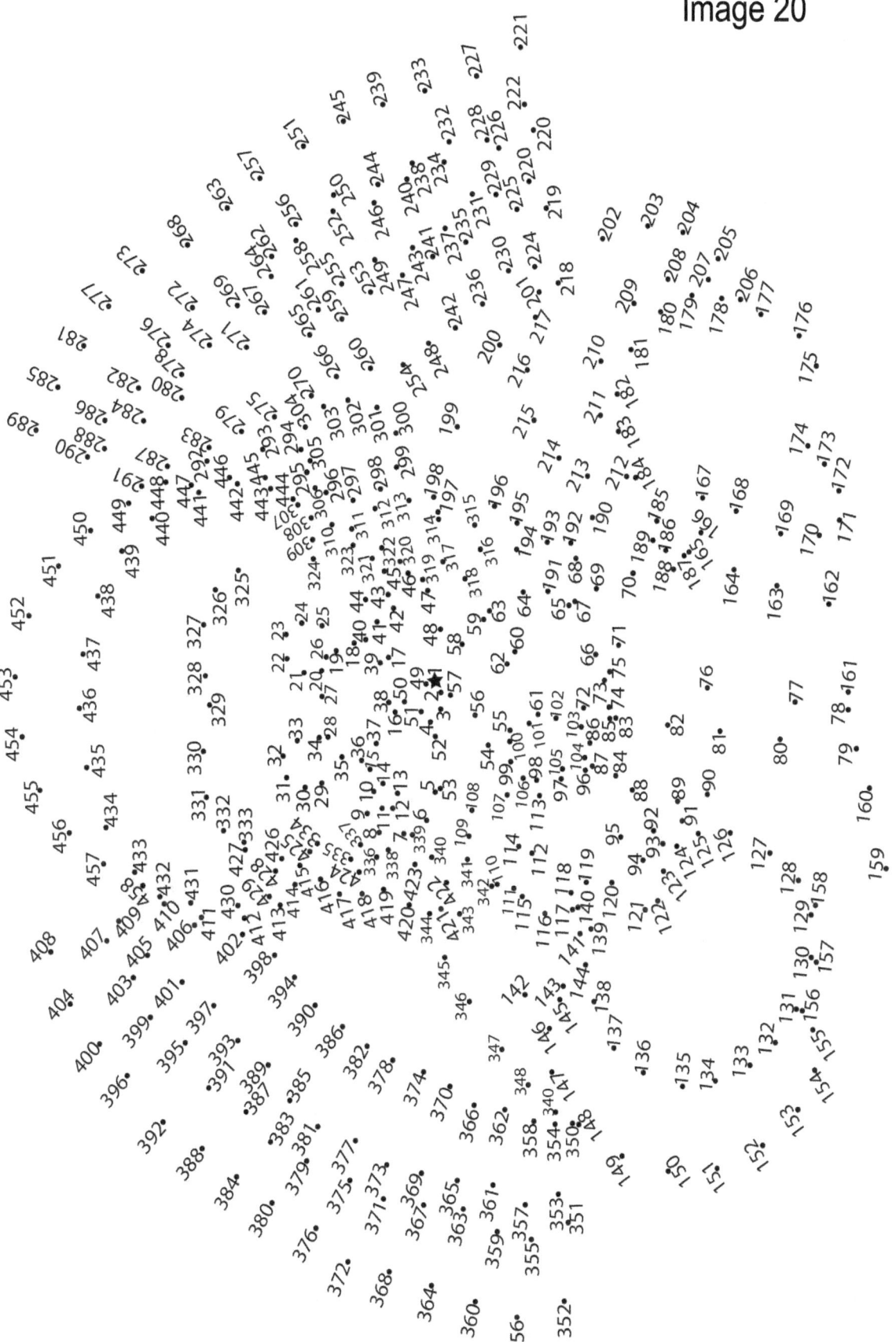

Image 20

Enjoy bonus images from
some of our other fun
dot-to-dot books

Find all of our books on Amazon

Easy to Read Large Print Dot to Dot
Beautiful Landscapes
Puzzles from 150 to 760 Dots

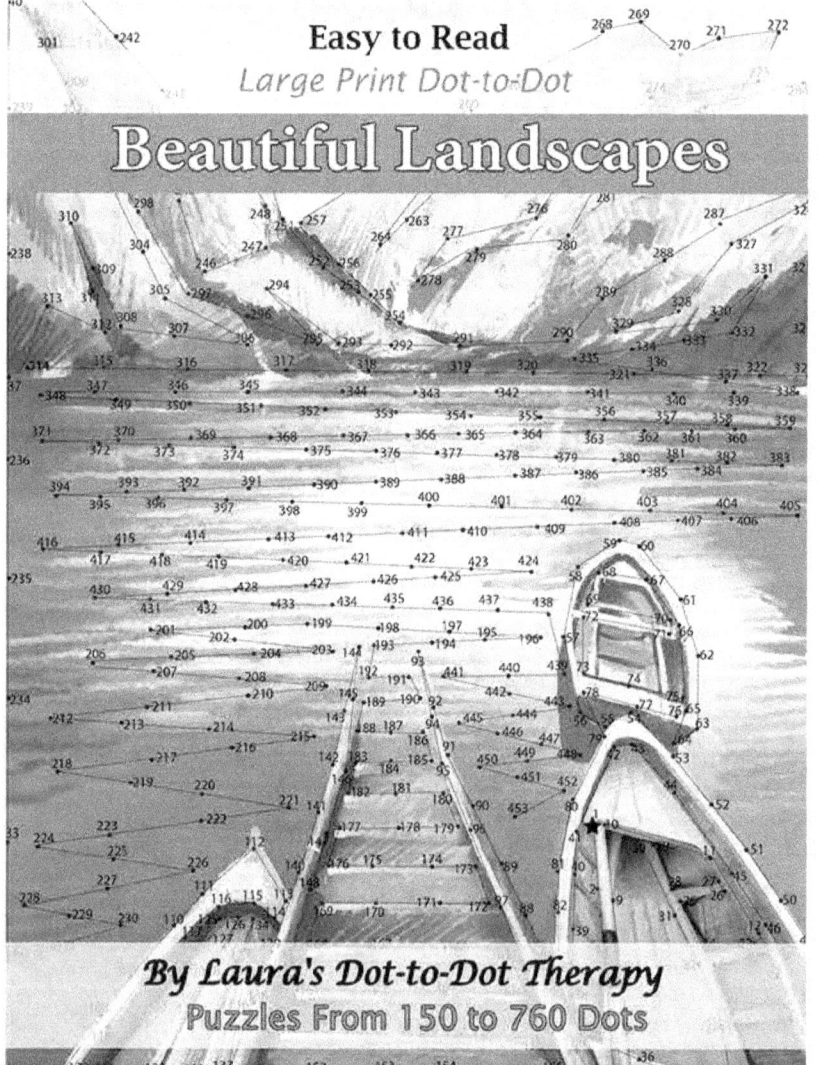

Antique Cars and Vintage Cars
Large Print Dot-to-Dot Book for Adults

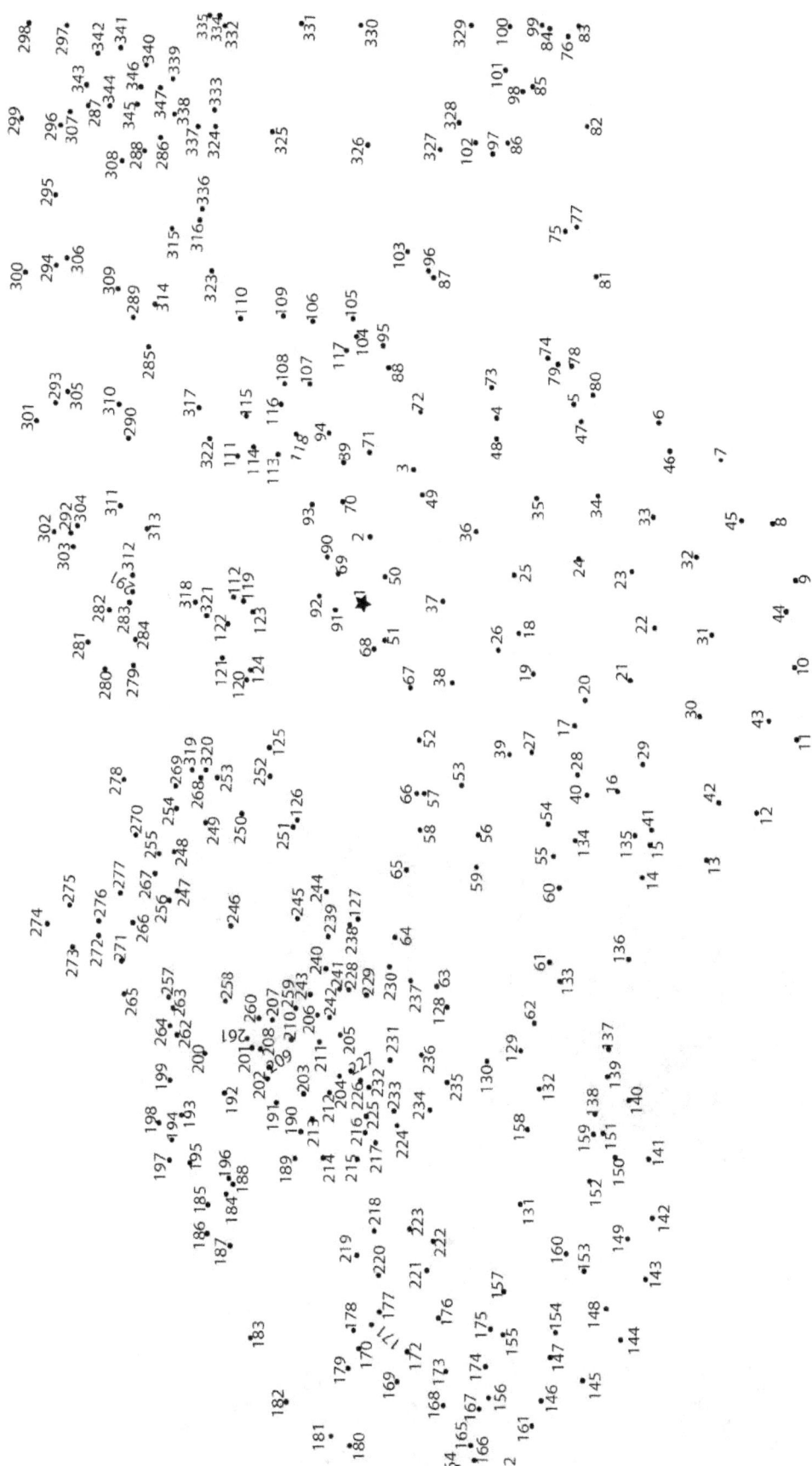

Famous Faces
Big Book of Extreme Dot to Dot

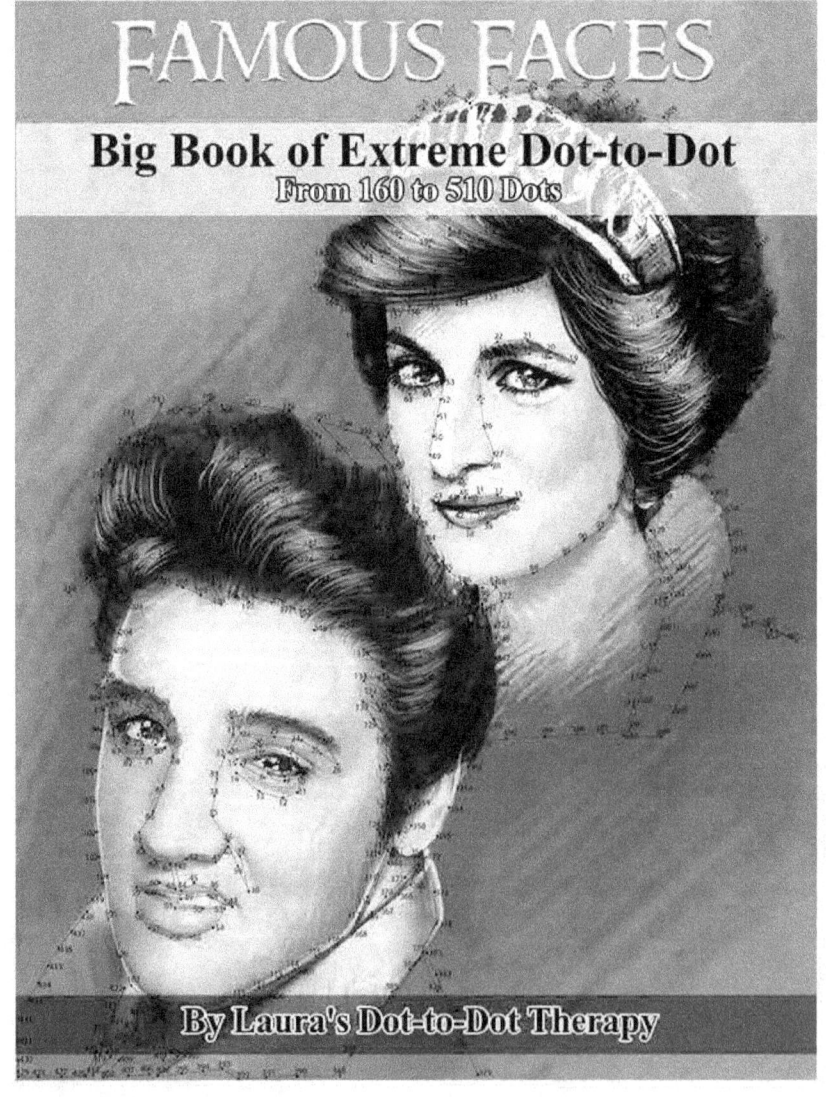

Mythical Mermaid
Dot-to-Dot Book for Adults
Puzzles from 150 to 750 Dots

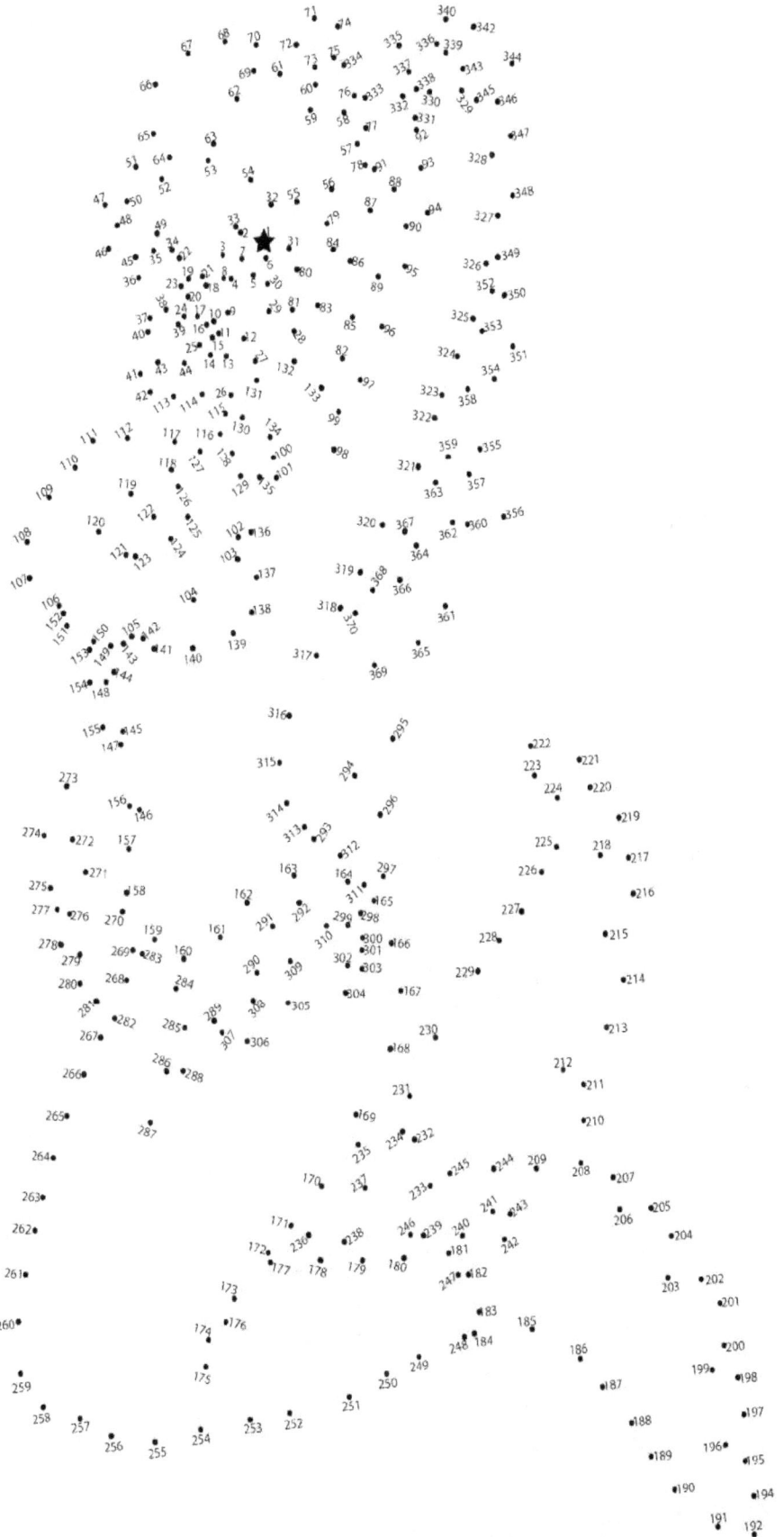

Unicorn, Dragons, and Magical Creatures
Dot-to-Dot Puzzles from 462 to 956 Dots

ANSWER KEY

Follow along with the
page numbers from top left
to bottom right

Image 1

Image 2

Image 3

Image 4

Image 5

Image 6

Image 7

Image 8

Image 9

Image 10

Image 11

Image 12

Image 13

Image 14

Image 15

Image 16

Image 17

Image 18

Image 19

Image 20